What Dress Makes of Us

Dorothy Quigley

Illustrated by Annie Blakeslee

WHAT DRESS MAKES OF US

By

DOROTHY QUIGLEY

Illustrations by

ANNIE BLAKESLEE

1897

I am indebted to the editors of the New York *Sun* and New York *Journal* for kindly allowing me to include in this book articles which I contributed to their respective papers.

PREFACE.

Did you ever observe, dear comrade, what an element of caricature lurks in clothes? A short, round coat on a stout man seems to exaggerate his proportions to such a ridiculous degree that the profile of his manly form suggests " the robust bulge of an old jug."

A bonnet decorated with loops of ribbon and sprays of grass, or flowers that fall aslant, may give a laughably tipsy air to the long face of a saintly matron of pious and conservative habits.

A peaked hat and tight-fitting, long-skirted coat may so magnify the meagre physical endowments of a tall, slender girl that she attains the lank and longish look of a bottle of hock.

Oh! the mocking diablery in strings, wisps of untidy hair, queer trimmings, and limp hats. Alas! that they should have such impish power to detract from the dignity of woman and render man absurd.

Because of his comical attire, an eminent Oxford divine, whose life and works commanded reverence, was once mistaken for an ancient New England spinster in emancipated garments. His smoothly shaven face, framed in crinkly, gray locks, was surmounted by a soft, little, round hat, from the up-turned brim of which dangled a broken string. His long frock-coat reached to just above his loosely fitting gaiters.

The fluttering string, whose only reason for being at all was to keep the queer head-gear from sailing away on the wind, gave a touch of the ludicrous to the boyish hat which, in its turn, lent more drollery than dignity to the sanctified face of the old theologian. Who has not seen just such, or a similar sight, and laughed? Who has not, with the generosity common to us all, concluded these were the mistakes and self-delusions of neighbors, relatives, and friends, in which we had no share?

I understand how it is with you. I am one of you. Before I studied our common errors I smiled at my neighbor's lack of taste, reconstructed my friends, and cast contemptuous criticism upon my enemies. One day I took a look at myself, and realized that " I, too, am laughable on unsuspected occasions."

The humbling knowledge of seeing myself objectively, gave me courage to speak to the heart of you certain home truths which concern us all, in homely language which we can all understand.

That you may discern the comicality and waggery in ill-chosen clothes, I have endeavored to hint to you in these talks some of the ways gew-gaws and garments make game of us.

May you discover that your dress is not making you a laughable object; but if, by any chance, you should note that your clothes are caricaturing you, take heart. Enjoy the joke with the mirth that heals and heartens, and speedily correct your mistakes.

The lines of your form, the modelling of your face, are they not worthy of your discerning thought? Truly! Whatever detracts from them detracts from sculpture, painting, and poetry, and the world is the loser.

A word to the thinking is sufficient.

D.Q.

CONTENTS.

CHAPTER I.

HOW WOMEN OF CERTAIN TYPES SHOULD DRESS THEIR HAIR.

The pleasing, but somewhat audacious statement of the clever writer who asserted, " In the merciful scheme of nature, there are no plain women," is not as disputable as it may seem. Honest husbands, to be sure, greet the information with dissenting guffaws; gay deceivers reflect upon its truth by gallantly assenting to it, with a mocking little twinkle in their eyes; and pretty women, upon hearing it, remark sententiously " Blind men and fools may think so." Discerning students of womankind, however, know that if every woman would make the best of her possibilities, physically, mentally, and spiritually, it would be delightfully probable that " in the merciful scheme of nature" there need be no plain women.

Have we not Lord Chesterfield's word for it, that " No woman is ugly when she is dressed" ?

It is no unworthy study to learn to make the best of, and to do justice to, one's self. Apropos of this, to begin—where all fascinating subjects should begin—at the head, it behooves every woman who wishes to appear at her best, to study the modelling of her face that she may understand both its defective and perfect lines. By a proper arrangement of her hair a woman can do much to obscure or soften her bad features, and heighten the charm of her good ones.

1

Romancers have written, and poets have sung, of the bewitchment in nut-brown locks, golden tresses, and jetty curls. Every woman, if so inclined, may prove for herself the transfiguring effect in a becoming coiffure. In fact, the beauty of a woman's face and her apparent age are greatly affected by the way she wears her hair.

A most important detail that too few consider, is, the proper direction in which to comb the hair. Women literally toss their tresses together without any attention to the natural inclination of the individual strands or fibres. They comb their hair " against the grain."   Those who do so never have beautifully and smoothly arranged coiffures. Each little hirsute filament has a rebellious tendency to go in the direction nature intended it should, and refuses to " stay where it is put,"   giving the head in consequence, an unkempt and what is termed an " unladylike"   appearance. The criss-cross effect resulting from combing and arranging the hair contrary to " the grain" is conspicuously apparent in the coiffure of no less a personage than Eleanora Duse, who, as may be seen from the picture, pays little attention to the natural tendency of the dark tresses that cover her shapely head. The bang has the dishevelled appearance of a pile of jack-straws. The side-locks instead of being combed or brushed to follow the contour of the head, fall loosely and fly in opposite directions.

NO. 2

French coiffeur.

The difference in appearance between the women of the smart sets in America and those of less fashionable circles is due, in a great measure, to the beautifully dressed coiffures of the former. A hair-dresser arranges, at least once a week, the hair of the modish woman if her maid does not understand the art of hair-dressing. Many women of the wealthy world have their maids taught by a

2

A wise woman will adopt a prevailing mode with discretion, for, what may be essentially appropriate for one, may be fatally inappropriate for another. In adjusting her " crown of glory" a woman must consider the proportions of her face. She should be able to discern whether her eyes are too near the top of her head or, too far below; whether she has a square or wedge-shaped chin; a lean, long face, or a round and bountifully curved one. She should be alert to her defects and study never to emphasize nor exaggerate them.

Why, through stupidity or carelessness, make a cartoon of yourself, when with a proper appreciation of your possibilities you can be a pleasing picture? It is just as glorious to be a fine picture or a poem as it is to paint the one, or write the other. Indeed, a woman who harmoniously develops the best within her has the charm of an exquisite poem and inspires poets to sing; and if by the grace and beauty of her dress she enhances her natural endowments and makes herself a pleasing picture, the world becomes her debtor.

In the important matter of becomingly arranging the hair, the following sketches and suggestions may hint to bright, thinking, women what styles to choose or avoid.

For Wedge-Shaped Faces.

The least-discerning eye can see that the wedge-Shaped face No. 3 is caricatured, and its triangular proportions made more evident, by allowing the hair to extend in curls or a fluffy bang on either side of the head. Women with delicately modelled faces with peaked chins should avoid these broad effects above their brows.

NO. 3

NO. 4

It is obvious in the sketch No. 4, that the wedge-shaped face is perceptibly improved by wearing the hair in soft waves, or curls closely confined to the head and by arranging a coil or high puff just above and in front of the crown. This arrangement gives a desirable oval effect to the face, the sharp prominence of the chin being counteracted by the surmounting puffs.

For Heavy Jaws.

It may readily be seen that a woman with the square, heavy-jawed face pictured by No. 5, should not adopt a straight, or nearly straight, bang, nor wear her hair low on her forehead, nor adjust the greater portion of her hair so that the coil cannot be seen above the crown of her head. The low bang brings into striking relief all the hard lines of her face and gives the impression that she has pugilistic tendencies.

NO. 5

To insure artistic balance to her countenance, and bring out the womanly strength and vital power of her face, her hair should be arranged in coils, puffs, or braids that will give breadth to the top of her head as shown by No. 6. A fluffy, softly curled bang adds grace to the forehead and gives it the necessary broadness it needs to lessen and lighten the heaviness of the lower part of the face. A bow of ribbon, or an aigrette of feathers, will add effectively the crown of braids or puffs which a wise woman with a square jaw will surmount her brow if she wishes to subdue the too aggressive, fighting qualities of her strong chin.

NO. 6

For Short Faces.

The sisterhood who have short, chubby faces should, in a measure, observe certain rules that apply in a small degree to those who have heavy chins.

As may be observed even with a casual glance, the little short-faced woman depicted by No. 7, causes her round facial disk to appear much shorter than it really is by allowing her hair to come so far down on her forehead. She further detracts from her facial charms by wearing " water-waves." Water-waves are scarcely

NO. 7

4

to be commended for any type of face, and they are especially unbecoming to the woman who is conspicuously " roly-poly." The round eyes, knobby nose, and round mouth are brought into unattractive distinctness by being re-duplicated in the circular effects of the hair. This mode of dressing the hair makes a short face look common and insignificant.

Do you not see that this type is immensely improved by the arrangement of the coiffure in No. 8? By combing her hair off her forehead her face acquires a look of alertness and intelligence, besides being apparently lengthened. She can wear her bang in soft crimps brushed back from her brow, if this plain arrangement is too severe.

NO. 8

For Eyes Set Too High.

A low forehead is supposed to be a sign of beauty in woman. The brows of the famous Venuses are low and broad. Perhaps for this reason many women wear their hair arranged low upon their foreheads. Whether the hair should be worn low on the brow depends chiefly on two things, —" the setting of the eyes, and the quality of the face."

A good rule to observe is the artistic one, to the effect that " the eyes of a woman should be in the middle of her head." That is, if an imaginary line were drawn across the top of the head and another below the chin, exactly midway between the two the eyes should be set.

The Japanese type of woman should carefully observe the foregoing hint.

NO. 8½.

NO. 9

Observe No. 8-1/2. Nature has not been artistic. The eyes are too near the top of the head. The defect is exaggerated and emphasized by the wearing of the hair low on the forehead. In some faces of this type the face is brutalized in appearance by this arrangement. The expression and whole quality of the countenance can be greatly improved by arranging the hair as shown by No. 9, which is the soft Pompadour style. The Duchess of Marlborough, formerly Consuelo Vanderbilt, frames her naïve, winsome face, which is of the Japanese type, in a style somewhat like this. Her dark hair forms an aureole above her brow, and brings into relief the dainty, oval form of her face. Even simply brushing the hair off the forehead without crimp or roll will improve the appearance of this type of face and give it a better artistic balance.

For Eyes Set Too Low.

Women whose eyes are set too far down in their faces should adopt a mode of arranging their hair exactly the opposite of those whose eyes are set too near the top of their heads.

It is apparent that No. 10 exaggerates the distance of her eyes from the crown of her head, and makes them appear to be set lower than they really are by building her hair high, and by brushing her bang back so severely from her brow. A bald forehead is rarely becoming to any woman. A few stray curls or soft

NO. 10

waves lend grace to even the most perfect of brows.

By bringing the hair down over the forehead, as suggested in No. 11, a woman with this type of face can easily improve her appearance. By this graceful arrangement her face loses the childish and sometimes stupid expression that is peculiar to the type, as may be discerned in No. 10. When the hair is properly

NO. 11

arranged this element of childlikeness lends a certain appealing sweetness not unattractive even in the faces of matured matrons. By dressing the hair low so the coil does not appear above the crown, as in No. 11, the eyes are apparently properly placed.

For Long Faces with Long Noses.

The woman who wears her silken tresses arranged on either side of her head, draped like curtains from a central parting, is to be envied if she can do it and yet look young and pretty. She is the Madonna type and seems to possess all the attributes of gentleness, modesty, and meekness, and angelic sweetness that are supposed to characterize the distinctively feminine woman. This is the ideal style of coiffure much bepraised by man, because, according to a bright modern Amazon, " it makes a woman look so meek."

The only type to which it is really becoming is the Italian. The type with *matte* complexion, soft eyes, finely chiselled nose, and delicately oval chin, look ideally sweet and feminine with the hair arranged *à la* Madonna.

Long faces of the form pictured by No. 12 exaggerate the longness and leanness of their faces by wearing their locks like looped curtains. A long nose with two long lines on either side of the cheek seems longer than it is, as the observer may discern three lines instead of only the nasal one, and the impression of longness is emphasized. Not only is the length of the countenance made more noticeable, but years and years are apparently added to the actual age.

That No. 13, which shows a parting and soft waves that do not come below the ears, is to be preferred by a woman whose features are of this character need hardly be explained. The improvement in looks is quite obvious.

No. 14 is an example of a misguided woman of the pudgy type who, for some inexplicable reason, arranges her hair in the Madonna style. It is utterly unsuited to her face. Unless her ears are deformed this style of hirsute lambrequins should not be worn by a full, round-faced woman. The arrangement sketched in No 15 adds effectively to her appearance, not only making her look younger, but less inane.

For Faces with Protruding Noses.

Women with decidedly protruding, or irregular, tip-tilted noses should be especially careful in arranging their coiffures.

Any woman who arranges her hair as in sketch No. 16 caricatures her facial defects by increasing the too protuberant lines of her nose. The distance from the end of her nose and the tip of the topmost knot of hair is too long for either beauty or intelligence. The shape of her

head acquires idiotic proportions, and her nose is placed entirely " out of drawing" and is obtrusively conspicuous when seen in profile. This type of woman is generally classified among the inquisitive, bright, and energetic. She should aim to modify the unhappy angularity of her profile as well as to repress her gossipy tendencies. The graduated coil of hair and waved coiffure, shown by No. 17, are most felicitous in their effect on this type of face.

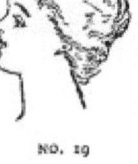

No. 18 reveals an error in an opposite direction. The snubbed-nose girl, by fixing her hair in a bun-like coil, gives the impression that her coiffure is held by invisible strings by her nose, which gets a more elevated look than it otherwise would have, because of the bad angle at which the coil is placed.

No. 19, which is a picturesque variation of the popular coif, manifestly improves this type of face, and makes the nose appear less obtrusive.

A woman should carefully study the contour of her head from every side; the modelling of her face; the length and inclination of her nose; the setting of her eyes; and the breadth and form of her brow, and adopt a becoming coiffure that will give artistic balance to her face, and never absolutely change the style whatever the mode in hair-dressing may be. In England, the court hair-dresser years ago studied the character of the head and face of the Princess of Wales, and designed a coiffure for her which she has never varied until recently; then she merely arranged her fringe lower down on her forehead than she has ever worn it before. The general style, however, she preserves intact, and wears her hair, and has for many years, as is shown in the picture—No. 20. Her daughters, who have faces the same shape as hers, dress their coiffures similarly. In never changing the style of arranging her hair, the Princess of Wales owes in no small degree her apparent air of youthfulness.

NO MATTER WHAT THE PREVAILING STYLE THESE RULES MAY BE PRACTICALLY APPLIED.

CHAPTER II.

HINTS FOR THE SELECTION OF BECOMING AND APPROPRIATE STYLES IN HEAD-GEAR.

Closely allied to the subject of hair-dressing is that of head-gear. Indeed many of the hints regarding appropriate coiffures for certain styles of faces are equally applicable to the selection of suitable hats and bonnets. The choosing of millinery is the more momentous of the two, of course, for I need scarcely remind you that Nature left us no choice in hair. No matter what its color or texture we desire to keep it and if we are wise we will make the best of it.

In regard to hats we are personally responsible and our follies are upon our own heads.

The power of caricature being greater in hats than in hair-dressing, is it not fit that we should give careful and intelligent consideration to the selection of our millinery that the ugly lines in our otherwise beautiful faces may not be at the mercy of mocking bunches of ribbons, comically tilted straws, or floppy bits of lace?

The Magic of The Bonnet.

Once upon a time, I think that was the exact date, there was a man distinguished in a certain kingdom as the ugliest person in the realm. According to a blithe romancer, he was so distinctively unpleasing in form and feature that he challenged the attention of the king who, in whimsical mood, made him a royal retainer. The man so conspicuously lacking in beauty enjoyed his eminent position and privileges for some time. But even ugliness, if it attain distinction, will excite envy in the low-minded. A former associate of the unbeautiful man in invidious temper brought the news one day to the king, that there was an old woman in his domain that was uglier than the lowly-born man who by kingly favor held so high a place. " Bring her to the court. Judges shall be called to decide. If she is uglier she shall stay and he shall go," was the royal mandate. When the old woman appeared she was easily decided to be by far the uglier of the two. At the critical moment when the king was upon the eve of dismissing the man from his retinue, a friend of the unfortunate shouted, " Put her bonnet on him!" This was done, and lo! a fearful change was wrought. By unanimous acclamation he was declared to be " the ugliest creature on earth."

The old woman, true to the instincts of her sex, refused to wear her bonnet again. Like many of her sisters of modern times, she had not before discovered the possibilities in a bonnet to enhance the beauty of the face or decrease its charms.

If woman could see themselves objectively, as did the old woman, they would keenly realize the necessity of considering the lines of hat or bonnet in relation to those of their faces, and would learn to obscure defects and bring into prominence their prettiest features.

As there are a few rules to govern what each type should select, every one of the fair sisterhood has an equal opportunity to improve her appearance by selecting in the millinery line the distinctive adornment suited to her individual style.

For Women with Broad Face and Heavy Chin.

By a curious law of contrariety the woman with a broad, heavy chin seems to have an ungovernable penchant for trig little round bonnets, or trim turbans with perky aigrettes, like that in sketch No. 22. By obeying this wilful preference she obscures whatever delicacy may be in the modelling of her features and brings into conspicuous relief the ugliest lines of her face. Her chin is apparently increased in heaviness and the broadness of her face is made prominent. She could easily have restored the artistic balance to her facial lines by wearing a large hat, rather heavily trimmed, as in No. 23, thus effectively modifying the strong curves of the chin and signally improving her appearance. If a woman's face is fairly proportioned, not too short for its breadth, and she can not afford plumes, this type of woman can still give a becoming balance to her face by adopting hats that are trimmed with flamboyant bows that

NO. 22

NO. 23

flare horizontally across the hat, diverging from a central knot in the from.

For the Woman with Tapering Chin.

NO. 25

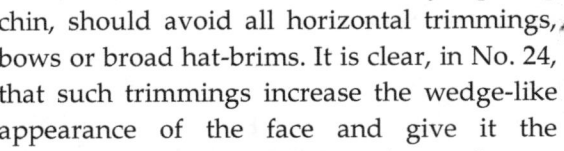

NO. 24

The woman who is the exact opposite of the type with the ample lower jaw, but whose chief disadvantage lies in her broad, manly brow and tiny tapering chin, should avoid all horizontal trimmings, bows or broad hat-brims. It is clear, in No. 24, that such trimmings increase the wedge-like appearance of the face and give it the grotesque suggestion of an ordinary flower-pot in which grows a sickly plant. This type can perceptibly improve upon nature by choosing the style of hat and neck-gear shown by No. 25.

The crinkly ovals that form the brim of the hat, and the soft, graceful arrangement of the hair in front that decreases the too broad effect of the brow, and the full fluffy ruff snuggled up closely to the chin, produce a pleasing transformation of the meagre-looking original that to the uninitiated seems little short of magical. The broad, cravat-like bows, and the flaring ones known as " incroyables," were beneficently wedge-like faces and throats that have lost the seductive curves of youth.

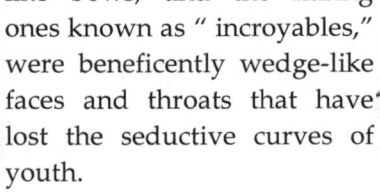

NO. 26

NO. 27

Hat for the Chubby Woman.

That amiable type of woman formed conspicuously upon the circular plan often unconsciously impresses the fact of her fatal tendency to rotundity by repeating the roundness of her globular eyes, the disk-like appearance of her snub nose and the circle of her round mouth, and the fulness of her face by wearing a little, round hat in the style portrayed by No. 26.

The curls of her bang, the feathers in her hat, the high collar of her jacket make more significant the fact that her lines are not artistic and that her face is unbeautifully round. She can enhance her charms and apparently decrease the too spherical cut of her countenance by adopting the mode illustrated in No. 27. The angular bows on the hat, the geometric lines of the broad hat-brim, the precise cut of the lapels on the corsage, the neat throat-band and V-shaped vesture— all insinuate in a most engaging way a dignity and fine, high-bred poise totally obliterated by the circular style of dress erroneously adopted by the misguided woman in No. 26.

For Women Who Have Sharp and Prominent Profiles.

In buying a hat many of the " unfair sex" —as the modern wag dubs the progressive sisters who wish to have all man's rights and privileges and keep their own besides—never seem to consider their heads but from a front point of view. In consequence, as sketch No 28 hints, a head seen from the side frequently appears, if not idiotically, very inartistically, proportioned.

NO. 28

NO. 29

Occasionally a hat presents as comical an effect in a from as in a side view, as may be seen in No. 29. The wearer was an elderly woman with gray hair which hung down in a half-curled bang on either side of her thin face. Her hat which was simply " dripping" with feathers suggested a fanciful letter " T" and exaggerated the thinness of her face in a remarkably funny way. The feathers overhanging the brim increased the broadness of the hat, and looked singularly waggish fluttering against the spriggy-looking projections of gray hair. The rules for the wedge-shaped face, as may readily be discerned, apply here.

Women who have sharp and prominently outlined profiles have a curious tendency to

13

choose hats, the brims of which project too far forward in front, and turn up too abruptly and ungracefully in the back.

As shown in No. 30 the protruding brim gives the head and face the unattractive proportions of the capital letter " F." The length of the nose is emphasized by the line of the hat-rim above it and it appears unduly obtrusive. The flat arrangement of the hair and the curve of the hat-brim in the back also exaggerate the obtrusive qualities of the features. By choosing a hat somewhat similar to the one sketched in No. 31, the unattractive sharpness of the profile is modified, and the alert, agreeable quality of the face, that was obscured by the shelf-like brim, becomes apparent. The observer feels, if he does not voice it, that it is a progressive spirit advancing forward instead of an ungainly head-piece that looks like a curious trowel.

For the Woman with an Angular Face.

The woman with the angular features presented in No. 32 should not wear a sailor-hat or any hat with a perfectly straight rim.

The sailor-hat or any style bordering on it should be selected with utmost discrimination. This mode is unbecoming to a woman more than forty; or, to one who through grief or worry prematurely attains a look of age, or to one whose features are irregular. The straight brim across the face is very trying. It casts a shadow deepening the " old marks" and instead of being a frame to set off, it seems to cut off, the face at an inartistic angle.

NOS. 32 AND 33

The woman with angular features, as may be seen by No. 33, can wear with impunity, and always should wear, a hat the brim of which is waved, turned, twisted, or curved in graceful lines. The uneven brim of her hat makes an effective complement to the angularity of her chin, which is further softened by the feathery ruff that encircles her throat. The curves of the ostrich plumes, and the studied carelessness of the arrangement of her coiffure, subdue the angles of her face which are brought out in unbecoming prominence by the sailor-hat.

Women Who should Not Wear Horns.

The velvet horns on either side of a hat, the steeple-like central adornments that were once much in favor, and the Mercury wings that ornament the coiffure for evening dress, produce some startling, disagreeable, and amusing effects not altogether uninteresting to consider.

Faces in which the eyes are set too near the forehead acquire a scared look by being surmounted by a bonnet upon which the trimming gravitates to a point in an arrangement not unsuggestive of a reversed fan, horns, or a steeple.

NO. 34

The most unpleasing developments result from the wearing of the horn-like trimmings either in velvet or jet. If the face above which they flare has less of the spiritual than the coarse propensities in it, the grotesque turns and twists in the head-gear emphasize the animality in the lines characteristic of low-bred tendencies, and the whole countenance is vulgarized. One face acquires the look of a fox, another of a certain type of dog, and so on.

The most amusing exaggerations of distinctive facial lines are produced by Mercury wings. The good-natured woman of the familiar type depicted in No. 34 brings every bovine attribute of her placid countenance into conspicuous relief by surmounting her face with the wings of the fleet-footed god. The cow-like form and serenity of her features are made laughably obvious.

Short, delicately-faced women can adorn their coiffures with Mercury wings with most charming results. Wings, or perpendicular bows, add length to the lines of the short face, giving it a certain suggestion of refinement and distinction that is wholly destroyed by the wearing of any trimmings that show at the sides.

NO MATTER WHAT THE PREVAILING STYLE THESE RULES
MAY BE PRACTICALLY APPLIED.

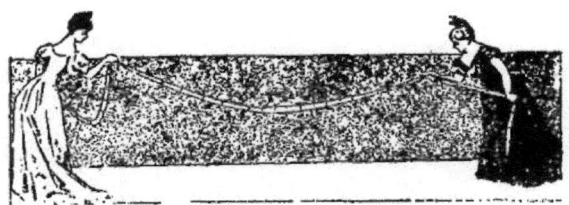

CHAPTER III.

LINES THAT SHOULD BE RECOGNIZED AND CONSIDERED IN MAKING COSTUMES.

Mme. La Mode, much misrepresented as are all who are embarrassed with world-wide popularity always considers when designing fashions that women vary in form, as in mood. She suits all needs, although this fact has never been cast to her credit. With a beautiful sense of adjustment—as obvious as that in Nature, that projects the huge watermelon to ripen on a slender vine on the ground and swings a greengage plum on the stout stem of a tree to mature in storm or shine—Mme. La Mode, arbiter of styles, balances her fashions.

Never came the big hat without the small bonnet. Accompanying the long cloak is the never-failing short cape. Side by side may be found the long coat and the short, natty jacket. This equilibrium in wearing apparel may be traced through all the vagaries of fashion.

Everybody's need has been considered, but everybody has not considered her need.

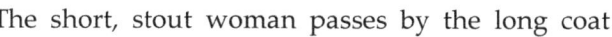

The short, stout woman passes by the long coat better adapted to her and seizes a short jacket—a homeopathic tendency of like suiting like, sometimes efficacious in medicine, but fatal in style.

Style for Tall Slender Woman.

The very tall, slender woman frequently ignores a jaunty jacket and takes a long coat like that shown in No. 36.

NOS. 36

AND 37

To even the sluggish fancy of an unimaginative

observer she suggests a champagne bottle, and to the ready wit she hints of no end of amusing possibilities for caricature.

The very tall woman should know that long lines from shoulder to foot give height, and she must discerningly strive to avoid length of line in her garments until she dons the raiment of the angels.

Horizontal lines crossing the figure seem to decrease height, and should be used as much as possible in the arranging and trimming of the tall woman's garments.

By selecting a shorter coat equally modish, as shown by No. 37, the too tall woman shortens her figure perceptibly.

The belt cuts off from her height in a felicitous way, and the collar, also horizontal, materially improves the size of her throat. The high collar, such as finishes the coat, in No. 36, adds to the length. Those who have too long arms can use horizontal bands on sleeves most advantageously.

The Coat the Short Stout Woman should Wear.

NOS. 38 AND 39

The short jacket that so graciously improved the appearance of the slender specimen of femininity is sinister in its effect on the short, stout woman, in sketch No. 38. It should be the study of her life to avoid horizontal lines. Length of limb is to be desired because it adds distinction. Her belt, the horizontal effect of the skirt of the jacket, the horizontal trimming of the bottom of the skirt, all apparently shortening her height, tend to make her ordinary and commonplace in appearance.

If her hips are not too pronounced she can wear the long coat, shown in picture No. 39. The V-shaped vesture gives her a longer waist, and the long lines of the revers add to the length of her skirt. If her hips are too prominent, she should avoid having any tight-fitting garments that bring the fact into relief. She should not wear the long coat, but she can effectively modify it to suit her needs, by only having a skirt, or tabs, or finishing straps in the back. If her jacket or basque is finished off with a skirt effect, it is best to have the little skirt swerve away just at the hip-line, half revealing and half concealing it.

The front should be made in a jacket effect, finishing just at the waist-line and opening over a blouse front that will conceal the waist-line. It is best for the too short, stout woman to obscure her waist-line as much as possible, to apparently give her increase of height.

To put the waist-line high up adds to length of limb, and, of course, is to be desired, but the fact that what is added below is taken from above the waist, should impel careful discrimination in the arrangement of this equatorial band.

The Cloak or Cape for a Tall Woman.

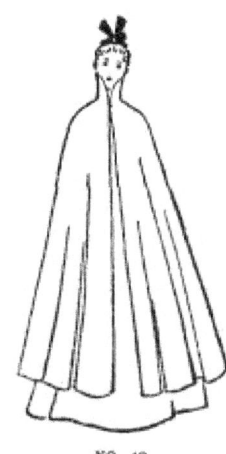

The long circular cloak is another graceful garment that can be worn with charming effect by the woman of classic height, but should never be in the wardrobe of a very tall woman except for use at the opera, when its service is chiefly required in the carriage, or when its wearer is sitting. It is so obvious, in sketch No. 40, that the vertical lines the folds of the cloak naturally fall into give a steeple-like appearance to the tall woman it enfolds, that it is scarcely necessary to comment upon it.

NO. 40

That her judicious selection should have been the short cape, which comes, as all capes should, to be artistic, well below the elbows, is clearly illustrated in picture No. 41. The horizontal trimming very becomingly plays its part in the generally improving effect.

NO. 41

The one who can wear the long cloak in an

19

unchallengeable manner is the short, stout woman, shown in sketch No. 42.

By wearing the short cape with circular, fluffy collarette, sketched in No. 43, she gives herself the look of a smothered, affrighted Cochin China chicken; or, as an imaginative school-girl remarked of her mother who wore a cape of similar style, " she looks as if her neck were encircled by bunches of asparagus."

NOS. 42 AND 43

The military dignity she acquires by wearing the long cape is becoming to a degree, and gives her distinction in form.

By remembering that horizontal trimmings apparently decrease the height, and that vertical lines add to it, those who desire to appear at their best will use discernment in dividing their basques with yokes, or corsage mountings at the bust-line or frills at the hip-line.

A flounce on the corsage at the bust-line, another at the hip-line, and yet another at the bottom of the shirt, increases the impression of bulkiness most aggressively and gives a barrel-like appearance to the form of a stout woman that is decidedly funny, as may be seen in sketch No. 44.

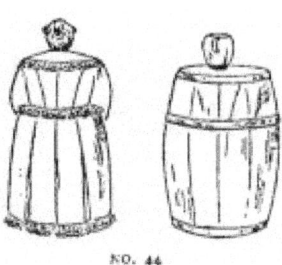

NO. 44

A study of the lines of the form will not only aid one in adopting a more becoming style of dress, but will sharpen the artistic perceptions, thus adding to the joy of life.

" A beautiful form is better than a beautiful face" and should be clothed so that its lines may appear at their best, and not be exaggerated and caricatured. The figure is seen many more times than the face, and the defects of the former are more conspicuous than those of the latter.

Do not be unjust to your beautiful body, the temple of your soul; above all, do not caricature it by selecting your clothes with indiscriminating taste.

NO MATTER WHAT THE PREVAILING MODE THESE RULES MAY BE PRACTICALLY APPLIED.

CHAPTER IV.

HOW PLUMP AND THIN BACKS SHOULD BE CLOTHED.

She was from the middle-West, and despite the fact that she was married, and that twenty-one half-blown blush roses had enwreathed her last birthday cake, she had the alert, quizzical brightness of a child who challenges everybody and everything that passes with the countersign—" Why?" She investigated New York with unabashed interest, and, like many another superior provincial, she freely expressed her likes and dislikes for its traditions, show-places, and people with a commanding and amusing audacity.

Her objections were numerous. The chief one that made a deep impression upon her metropolitan friends was her disapproval of Sarah Bernhardt's acting. The middle-Westerner, instead of becoming ecstatic in her admiration, and at a loss for adjectives at the appearance of the divine Sarah, merely perked at the great French artist for some time and then demanded, querulously: " What's the matter with her? Why does she play so much with her back to the audience? I don't like it."

It was a shock to the adorers of Sarah Bernhardt to hear her so irreverently criticised. They loyally united in her defence, and sought to squelch the revolter by loftily explaining that the actress turned her back so often to the audience because she had such a noble, generous nature and desired to give the other actors a chance. " She lets them take the centre of the stage, as they say in the profession," remarked one of the party, who prided herself upon being versed in the *argot* of the theatre.

" But she plays with her back to the audience when she is speaking and acting, and everybody else on the stage is still but herself," petulantly insisted the Western Philistine, showing no signs of defeat.

The situation was not wholly agreeable. The worshippers of Sarah could say nothing more in justification of her turning her back on them, but, with true feminine logic, concluded, " If Sarah Bernhardt

22

turns her back on the audience it is right, and that is all there is to say."

Just at this dramatic moment a voice from the adjoining row providentially interposed. The voice belonged to a well-known exponent of physical culture, who was never so happy as when instructing the intellectually needy. She said: " I will tell you why she plays with her back towards the audience more than any other actress upon the stage to-day." The middle-Westerner, no less impressed than her metropolitan friends, listened eagerly.

The exponent of straight backs and high chests explained didactically: " The back is wonderfully expressive; indeed it is full of vital expression. Bernhardt knows this better than any other actress because she has studied statuary with the passion of a sculptor, and because she understands that, not only the face, but the entire physical structure, is capable of expressing dramatic emotions. Strong feeling and action may be strikingly revealed by the back. Imprecations, denunciations, even prayers, seem to be charged with more force when an actress delivers them with her back turned, or half-turned to the audience.

" Bernhardt's back expresses a storm of fury when she imprecates vengeance," said the voice of authority. " Not only on the stage is the expression of the back discernible, and a knowledge of its character valuable, but in every-day life in drawing-room and street. How many women consider their backs when they dress? Look at

the backs here deformed by laces and fallals," she went on contemptuously. " The majority of women never look below their chins and I believe not one in ten ever looks thoughtfully at her back," she said emphatically.

NO. 45

The dramatic value of a well-poised, expressive back may only concern the thousands of young women who are aspiring to be a Sarah Bernhardt or a Rachel; but a knowledge of what constitutes a properly and artistically clothed back should be of interest to all women in civilized countries.

That there is much truth in the assertion that " the majority of women never look below their chins, and not one in ten ever looks thoughtfully at her back," every observer of womankind might testify.

The open placket-hole and sagging waist-band, sketched in No. 45, is an all too familiar sight that advertises the fact that too few women take even a cursory look at their backs. Fathers and brothers who wish to protect their womankind from adverse criticism frequently give impromptu lectures upon this very subject, as this slovenly arrangement of skirt and basque is not only seen in Grand Street, Second Avenue, and equally unfashionable quarters, but in Fifth Avenue where the modish set are *en évidence*. If the dainty safety-pin displayed in

NO. 46

No. 46, goes out of vogue, the time-honored custom of sewing hooks to the waist-band of the dress, is always in fashion. Indeed, many women prefer this way of connecting separate skirt and waist to using a conspicuous pin. This is almost too trivial a detail to discourse upon, but it is as true that details make dress as it is that " trifles make life" —and neither life nor dress is a trifle.

NO. 46½

The offence in No. 45 is more the result of untidiness than of a lack of artistic discrimination. Nos. 46-1/2 and 47, on the contrary, outrage the laws of art, and display ignorance of the value and beauty of lines.

No. 46-1/2 might serve to conceal a deformity of the shoulders. That really seems its only excuse for being. The full, ugly, straight pleat that falls to just below the waist-line lends neither grace nor style to the figure. It is too short to give the distinction and dignity that handsome wraps with long lines almost invariably do, although they seem to add

NO. 47

age to the form. There is a hint of youth in this ungraceful jacket to be sure, but it is not especially attractive in its suggestion of youthfulness.

No. 47, with a line at the neck-band, crossed bands in the centre of the shoulders, and lines across the back, is obviously inartistic. The back of a Venus, even, would be detracted from by such criss-crossed effects. Happy the woman who has so shapely a back she can afford to allow her waist to fit smoothly and plainly, unbroken by any conspicuous lines. If bands must be used to remedy the deficiencies of ungenerous Nature, let them be at the neck and waist; and if the back is unconscionably long, a band, or fold, or ruffle across the shoulders is to be commended.

No. 48 reveals a glaring error frequently made by the thin sisterhood. A tall, slender woman with a long waist, should not emphasize her length of lines by wearing pointed or V-shaped effects. The V-shaped arrangement, either in cut or trimmings, apparently increases her " longness and leanness." She should aim to

NO. 48

NO. 49

shorten her waist instead of lengthening it as the basque finished with a point obviously does. The drooping sleeves elongate her shoulder-lines, and bring into clearer relief her meagre proportions. She can easily improve her appearance by adopting either style of gown portrayed by Nos. 49, or 50. The broad belt at the waist-line in No. 49, and the flamboyant lace or braided piece

that adorns the shoulders, perceptibly adds to her breadth and decreases her length.

No. 50 is a felicitous cut for a street dress for a slim sister. The jaunty bloused waist smartly

NO. 50

NO. 51

conceals deficiencies in fine points.

The tall, thin sisterhood should eschew pointed effects and study to attain apparent breadth by using trimmings arranged horizontally. Bands of velvet, braid in waved lines, ruffles, and not too deeply cut scallops, may be used effectively by the very slender, who sometimes appear as if they are " without form and void," as the earth was " in the beginning."

No. 51 is an exposition of the mistake made by the sturdy sisterhood of stout and pendulous proportions. It is plain to be seen that the fluffy ruche at the throat-band, and the ruffle at the shoulder, and the spreading bow at the waist, and the trimmed sleeves, add bulkiness to a form already too generously endowed with flabby rotundity. Corpulent women must forego the swagger little basques or any sort of short, flounced effects below the waist-line.

Nos. 52 and 53 are eminently adapted to the matron of ample dimensions. One observer of beauty-giving effects has not unadvisedly called the waist-line " the danger-line." A stout sister, above all others, should not accentuate the waist-line. She should conceal it as much as possible. The coat back of No. 52 apparently lengthens the waist.

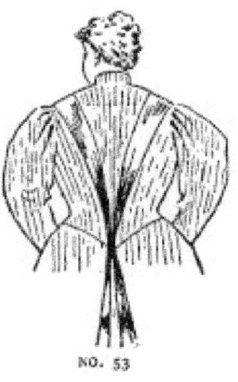

NO. 52

NO. 53

The same effect is produced by the arrangement of ribbons in No. 53, and by the long-pointed basque. V-shaped effects and long-pointed basques are as becoming to those burdened with flesh as they are unbecoming to tall, thin women.

Long, graceful folds and draperies are admirable for the stout sisterhood, who should avoid short sacques and tight-fitting garments that give the on-looker an uncomfortable impression; there is too much in a small space. Very light colors and thin textures that billow and float should be eschewed by the large, fleshy woman who wishes to give the impression that she possesses the lines of a finely modelled statue. She should avoid puffs and any suggestion of the pulpy and clumsy, and be careful not to sub-divide the body of her dress by plaits or braids laid on horizontally across or above the bust, or below the hips. Horizontal lines invariably decrease the height; for that reason stout women should not wear dresses cut square in the neck, but should adhere to the graceful V-or heart-shaped cut which has a tendency to give length.

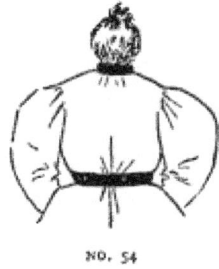

NO. 54

NO. 55

The rotund woman with a short waist, sketched in No. 54, may improve her figure, as shown in No. 55, by choosing belts and collars the exact shade of her shirt-waists in summer, and by not cutting off her height by any sort of outside belt on winter gowns.

Tall, stout women should forego high heels on their shoes, high hats, and striped dresses. Although stripes increase the effect of height, they also add to that of breadth. A plain cloth basque and skirt of striped material make a happy compromise and can be worn with becoming effect by a stout woman.

A basque cut high behind and on the shoulders apparently gives height.

NO. 56

A very stout woman should never wear double skirts or tunics or dresses with large sprawling patterns, such as depicted by cut No. 56, which suggests furniture stuffs. A large woman who had a fancy for wearing rich brocades figured with immense floral designs was familiarly called by her kind friends " the escaped sofa."

White, or very light colors, should never be worn by the stout; they greatly increase the apparent size. Large plaids should also be eschewed. Small checks and plaids may sometimes be becoming.

Neither the too thin nor the too stout should adopt a style of gown that caricatures the form as does the voluminous wrapper, finished with a box-pleat, as shown in No. 57. There is no grace in straight lines.

NOS. 57 AND 58

No. 58, which accentuates the height of the over-tall, thin woman, is better adapted to enhance the charms of a woman of finer proportions. The bony and scrawny, of the type of No. 58, seem to have a perverse desire to wear what makes their poverty in physical charms only more conspicuous. A woman of distinction in Boston, who is exceedingly thin and tall, wore Watteau pleats so frequently, even on reception and evening gowns that she was dubbed by a wag " the fire-escape," a title which so strikingly characterized her style, that the term was adopted by all her friends when they exchanged confidences concerning her.

The garment with the Watteau pleat is not unlike the princesse gown which is a very trying style except to handsomely proportioned women. A tall, well-developed woman, such as shown in sketch No. 59, adorns the princesse gown and attains in it a statuesque beauty. In suggesting statuary it fulfils the true ideal of dress, which should hint of poetry, art, sculpture, painting. The massing of colors; the arrangement of lines, the quality of textures, the grace and poise of the wearer—do not these hint of picture, statue, music?

CHAPTER V.

CORSAGES APPROPRIATE FOR WOMEN WITH UNBEAUTIFULLY MODELLED THROATS AND SHOULDERS.

Despite the traditional belief that a décolleté corsage is a tyrannous necessity of evening dress, a woman not graciously endowed with a beautifully modelled throat and shoulders may, with perfect propriety, conceal her infelicitous lines from the derisive gaze of a critical public.

Women are indebted to that gentle genius, La Duse, for the suggestion that a veiled throat and bust may charmingly fulfil the requirements of evening dress, and also satisfy that sense of delicacy peculiar to some women who have not inherited from their great-great-grandmothers the certain knowledge that a low-necked gown is absolutely decorous.

The women who does not possess delicate personal charms commends herself to the beauty-loving by forbearing to expose her physical deficiencies. Unless it is because they are enslaved by custom, it is quite incomprehensible why some women will glaringly display gaunt proportions that signally lack the exquisite lines of firm and solid flesh.

NO. 61

A throat like a ten-stringed instrument, surmounting square shoulders that end in knobs that obtrude above unfilled hollows, is an unpleasing vision that looms up conspicuously too often in opera-box and drawing-room.

The unattractive exhibition 61, is a familiar sight in the social world. How insufferably ugly such uncovered anatomy appears in the scenery of a rich and dainty music-room may be readily imagined by those

NO. 62

who have been spared the unpleasing display. It is so obvious that shoulders like these should always be covered that it seems superfluous to remark that this type should never wear any sleeve that falls below the shoulder-line.

The sleeve falling off the shoulder was invented for the classic contour, set forth in No. 62. Nor ribbons, nor lace, nor jewel are needed to enhance the perfect beauty of a fine, slender, white throat, and the felicitous curves of sloping shoulders.

One whose individual endowments are as meagre as are those presented in No. 61 may improve her defects by adopting either style of corsage, shown in sketches Nos. 63 and 64.

A woman's throat may lack a certain desirable roundness, and her shoulders may recede in awkward lines, and yet between these defective features the curves may have a not unpleasing daintiness and delicacy in modelling that can be

NO. 63   NO. 64

advantageously revealed. A modish velvet throat-band, such as is shown by No. 63, is one of the most graceful conceits of fashion. The too slim throat encircled by velvet or ornamented with a jewelled buckle or brooch is effectively framed. The unsightly lines of the shoulders are covered, and just enough individual robustness is disclosed to suggest with becoming propriety the conventional décolleté corsage. The Princess of Wales is as constant to her velvet or pearl neck-band, as to her especial style of coiffure. Her throat, in evening dress, never appears unadorned by one or the other of these beautiful bands that so cleverly conceal defects and seem to bring out more richly the texture and coloring of handsome bare shoulders.

Those who do not approve of the décolleté style of dress, or whose ungraceful proportions might well be entirely concealed, can wear with appropriateness and benefit the corsage shown in No. 64. This has much in its favor for a slender body. The upper part of the waist may be made of chiffon or crêpe, which is beautifully—one might say benignly—translucent. It has an insinuating transparency that neither reveals nor conceals too much. The neck-band of velvet or satin, full and soft, apparently enlarges the throat. The sleeves may be in whatever style in cut prevails. This costume carries perfectly into effect the requirements of evening dress, and may be worn with equal fitness to formal functions or to informal affairs. A coat-sleeve of lace, crêpe, or chiffon, beflounced at the wrist, may be inserted under the short satin sleeves when the occasion does not require gloves. The soft, white setting of thin textures around the throat and shoulders clears the complexion and brings into relief the pretty, delicate lines of a refined face.

NOS. 65 AND 66

It is plain to be seen that the unattractive specimen of femininity, No. 65., with the long, wrinkled neck and sharply lined face is unbecomingly costumed in the V-shaped basque and corsage which apparently elongate her natural lankness. A charming and always fashionable yoke-effect that she can wear to advantage is shown by No. 66. This style of corsage is equally effective for a too thin or a too muscular neck. The filling is of tulle.

A square-cut corsage is most becoming to the woman whose narrow shoulders have a consumptive droop. The angular cut apparently heightens the shoulders and decreases their too steeple-like inclination. The round cut, if it frames a full throat, is also an effective style for sloping shoulders. The V-shaped cut is most becoming to the short-necked woman, whose aim should be to increase the length of her throat.

NO. 68

NO. 67

It is not only the too thin neck that needs to be clothed with discrimination. Throats and shoulders that are too robust are improved by being covered. The arms and shoulders, however, are often the chief beauty of a fleshy woman, and it is to her advantage to give them as effective a setting as possible.

As is obvious in No. 67, the stout woman apparently increases her breadth by wearing a flamboyant corsage, and she hides the most exquisite lines of her arm with her sleeves.

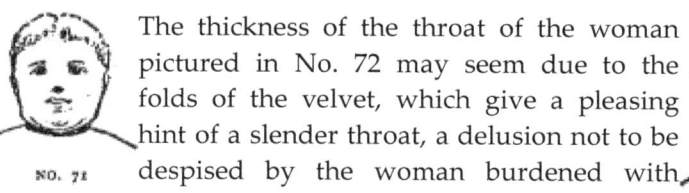

The princesse style of gown, in No. 68, gives her apparent length of waist. The modest lace flounce that falls in vertical folds decreases her formidable corsage. The knotted twist of silk reveals the full beauty of her arm.

In dressing the throat there are a few rules to be remembered. A too long, stem-like neck may be apparently shortened by a standing ruff or a full, soft band of velvet. The tight, plain band of velvet should never be worn by a woman with a very slim neck, as is plainly discernible in sketch No. 69.

NO. 69

NO. 70

The plain, military collar emphasizes the thinness of the slender woman's throat; but the soft crushed fold of velvet apparently enlarges the pipe-like proportions of the thin woman's neck, as may be seen in sketch No. 70. The tight-fitting collar should not be worn by the corpulent woman with a thick neck, as is shown by sketch No. 71.

The thickness of the throat of the woman pictured in No. 72 may seem due to the folds of the velvet, which give a pleasing hint of a slender throat, a delusion not to be despised by the woman burdened with flesh.

NO. 71

NO. 72

All the sisterhood,—stout, thin, long-throated, or short,—should know the hour when the withering touch of age begins to shrink the soft, round curves distinctive of the full, sweet throat of healthful youth. No regretful vanity should be allowed to glamour their eyes to the fact that Time has them by the throat, to put it melodramatically. The wise woman will not please herself with a fatal delusion. She will realize it is illusion she needs-yards of it— lace or velvet, or any beautifying texture that will conceal the deadly lines of age.

CHAPTER VI.

HINTS ON DRESS FOR ELDERLY WOMEN.

Dress has much to do with a youthful or aged appearance. Shawls and long mantles that fall from the shoulders give even youthful figures a look of age, because the lines are long and dignified and without especial grace. Beautiful wraps, or coats that do not come very far below the hip-line, can be worn becomingly by elderly ladies, neither emphasizing their years nor making them appear too frivolously attired. There is a smack of truth in the maxim, *As a woman grows old the dress material should increase in richness and decrease in brightness*. Handsome brocades, soft, elegant silks, woollen textures, and velvets are eminently suitable and becoming to women who are growing old.

Black, and black-and-white, soft white chiffon veiled in lace, cashmeres, and such refined tissues should be selected by those in " the first wrinkles of youth." Grays combined with filmy white material, dull bronzes lightened with cream-tinted lace, are also charmingly appropriate. Pale blue veiled in chiffon is another grateful combination.

White should be worn more than it is by old ladies. It is so suggestive of all that is clean, bright, and dainty; and if there is anything an old lady should strive to be in her personal appearance it is dainty. Exquisite cleanliness is one of the most necessary attributes of attractive old age, and any texture that in its quality and color emphasizes the idea of cleanliness should commend itself to those in their " advanced youth."

Little old thin women, large ones too, for that matter, who are wrinkled and colorless, should not wear diamonds. The dazzling white gems with pitiless brilliancy bring out the pasty look of the skin. The soft glow of pearls, the cloudlike effects of the opal, the unobtrusive lights of the moonstone harmonize with the tints of hair and skin of the aged.

Elderly women should not wear bright flowers on their bonnets or hats. Fresh-looking roses above a face that has lost its first youthfulness only make that fact more obvious. Forget-me-nots, mignonettes, certain pretty white flowers, the palest of pink roses, or the most delicate tint of yellow veiled with lace are not inappropriate for those who do not enjoy wearing sombre bonnets and hats which are composed only of rich, black textures. Lace cleverly intermingled with velvet and jewelled ornaments of dull, rich shades are exceedingly effective on the head-gear of the old.

Those who are gray-haired—and indeed all women as they grow old—should wear red above their brows instead of under their chins. A glint of rich cardinal velvet, or a rosette of the same against gray hair is beautiful.

Lace! Lace! Lace! and still more Lace for the old. *Lace is an essential to the dress of a woman more than forty years of age.* Jabots, ruches, yokes, cascades, vests, and gowns of lace, black or white, are all for the old. Rich lace has an exquisitely softening effect on the complexion. Thin women with necks that look like the strings of a violin should swathe, smother, decorate, and adorn their throats with lace or gossamer fabrics that have the same quality as lace. These airy textures, in which light and shadow can so beautifully shift, subdue roughnesses of the skin and harshness in lines. Old Dame Nature is the prime teacher of these bewitching artifices. Note her fine effects with mists and cobwebs, with lace-like moss on sturdy old oaks, the bloom on the peach and the grape. Nature produces her most enchanting colorings with dust and age. Laces, gauzes, mulls, chiffons, net, and gossamer throw the same beautiful glamour over the face and they are fit and charming accompaniments of gray hair, which is a wonderful softener of defective complexions and hard facial lines.

Too much cannot be written upon the proper arrangement in the neck-gear of the aged. The disfiguring wrinkles that make many necks unsightly may be kept in obeyance by massaging. No matter what the fashion in neck-gear, the aged must modify it to suit their needs. An old lady with a thin, pipe-stem neck should adopt a full ruche and fluffy, soft collar-bands. I cannot forbear repeating that tulle as light as thistle bubbles, either white or gray or black, is exquisitely effective for thin, scrawny necks. The fleshy, red neck should be softened with powder and discreetly veiled in chemisettes of chiffon and delicate net.

Old ladies may keep in the style, thus being in the picture of the hour; but it is one of the divine privileges of age that it can make its own modes. Absolute cleanliness, cleanliness as exacting as that proper nurses prescribe for babies, is the first and most important factor in making old age attractive. Rich dress, in artistic colors, soft, misty, esthetic, comes next; then the idealizing scarfs, collars, jabots, and fichus of lace and tulles. Old people becomingly and artistically attired have the charm of rare old pictures. If they have soul-illumined faces they are precious masterpieces.

CHAPTER VII.

HOW MEN CARICATURE THEMSELVES WITH THEIR CLOTHES.

Although in the dress of man there are fewer possibilities of caricature than in that of woman, yet, " the masterpieces of creation" frequently exaggerate in a laughable—and sometimes a pitiable— way, certain physical characteristics by an injudicious choice of clothes.

As the fashion in hair-dressing does not grant man the privilege of enhancing his facial attractions; nor of obscuring his defects by a becomingly arranged coiffure; and, as the modes in neck-gear are such that he cannot modify the blemishes of a defective complexion by encircling his athletic or scrawny throat with airy tulle, or dainty lace, that arch-idealizer of pasty-looking faces; and as he has forsworn soft, trailing garments that conceal unclassic curves and uninspiring lines of nether limbs, it behooves him to be more exactingly particular even than woman in the selection of his wearing apparel.

Far be it from me, however, to remind man of his many limitations— in dress. That he can never know the rapture of donning a becoming spring bonnet, nor the pleasure of possessing " real lace" things, nor the sensuous charm of being enwrapped in caressing furs, or sleazy, silken garments as exquisite in color and texture as beautiful, fresh flowers, only delicate consideration for his feelings constrains me from expatiating upon at length.

I would rather be able to remind him that he can make his limitations his advantages, than reveal to him what he misses in not being a woman.

To treat of this important subject adequately and convincingly, one would require the masterly discernment of a skillful and accomplished tailor, the experienced knowledge of a well-dressed man, and the alertly critical perception of a loving woman who, even in the matter of clothes, wishes the dearest of men to her, to do full justice to himself and her ideal of him on all occasions.

Although certain of the foregoing qualifications must needs be lacking, nevertheless this timorous pen, with more trepidation than courage it must be confessed, begs to call attention to a few obvious details in masculine attire that caricature, more or less, peculiarities in the forms and features of men.

To be sure, in the matter of head-gear man is not conspicuously at the mercy of burlesquing ribbons, flowers, and feathers, and he has fewer opportunities than women to make himself ridiculous, yet a few suggestions regarding certain shapes of head-gear for certain types of faces, applicable to women are equally applicable to him.

NO. 75

The same rule that applies to the women of the wedge-shaped type of face applies to the man of the wedge-shaped type, as may be seen in sketches Nos. 75 and 76. It is obvious that the youth depicted in No. 75 detracts from the

NO. 76

manliness of his face and emphasizes the pointed appearance of his countenance by wearing a hat with a broad brim projecting over his ears. This style of hat appears more frequently in straw than in any other texture, but the effect of a wide, projecting rim is the same in any material. No. 76, it is plain, improves the appearance of the long, slim-faced man. An alpine hat would not be unbecoming to him, the high oval of the crown forming a balance for the lower part of the face.

The man with a pugilistic chin should endeavor to select a hat that will not make his heavy jaw as prominent as does the stiff derby, in No. 77.

A soft alpine hat, or one somewhat of the style of No. 78, improves his appearance. The high crown and wide, gracefully rolling brim counter-balance the weight and prominence of the jaw.

NO. 77

Apropos of the minor details of man's garments, the button as a feature of clothes

NO. 78

has never been fully done justice to. It is a sustaining thing we know, something we can hang to, fasten to, and even tie to. That properly placed buttons contribute to our mental poise and therefore to our physical repose, is hinted in that absurdly engaging story, anent the smart boy who was the envy of his spelling-class, because he always stood first. You remember, no doubt, that an envious but keen-eyed classmate observed that the smart speller worked off his nervous apprehensiveness by twirling the top button of his coat as he correctly spelled word after word, day in and day out; and how the keen-eyed one played the part of a stealthy villain and surreptitiously cut the button off the coat. And do you remember the dramatic ending? How the smart one on the fatal day sought to " press the button" and finding it gone, lost his wits completely and failed ignominiously? Many of us when we have lost a sustaining button, have we not felt as ridiculously helpless and witbenumbed as the smart speller?

We all sub-consciously acknowledge our dependence upon buttons, but not many of us, evidently, have observed that even buttons have a certain possibility of caricature in them; and that they may add to, or detract from, the appearance of manly forms. The consideration of properly placed buttons may seem trivial to you, but if you will observe sketches Nos. 79 and 80, you may discern that a thin man may apparently increase his breadth and add a certain manly touch to his figure, by changing the buttons at line of his coat. The waist-buttons placed so near together, in No. 79, really make his toothpick proportions too obvious. His back is made to look broader by placing the buttons wider apart, as shown in No. 80, and changing the cut of his coat-tail.

NO. 79

NO. 80

NO. 81

NO. 82

That the fat man may also present a more attractive back to his enemies by considering the placing of his buttons, may be seen in drawings Nos. 81 and 82. The buttons decorating No. 81 are placed so far apart that they increase in an ungainly way the breadth of the back at the waist-line. If they are placed nearer together, and the seams graduated to meet them, they give the illusion of better and more desirable proportions, as may be seen in No. 82.

That the thin man may also present a more imposing and broader front to the world, is suggested in sketches Nos. 83 and 84. The contracted look of the coat in No. 83 is somewhat due to the buttons of his double-breasted coat being placed too closely together. The slender man who wishes to give the impression of being broad-chested may have the buttons on his coat placed a little farther apart than fashion may allow, as shown in sketch 84. The proportions may be easily preserved by a careful adjustment of the shoulder-seams and the seams under the arms.

NO. 83

NO. 84

The waist-line is not so much " a danger line" to man as to woman, yet man should not wholly ignore his equator. If he is long-waisted he can apparently balance his proportions by having his skirt shortened, as in No. 85, and his waist-line raised the merest bit. If he is too short-waisted he can lengthen his skirt and lower his waist-line, as shown in No. 86. In the one he escapes appearing too long and lanky in body, and in the other he obscures a lack of becoming inches that tends to give him a dumpy appearance.

NO. 85

NO. 86

If you study your fellow-men you will observe that few are really perfectly proportioned. One man will have the

body of a viking on the legs of a dwarf, or one will have the legs of an Apollo supporting the short body of a pigmy. The man who has a kingly body, too broad in proportion to his legs, as shown in sketch No. 87, should endeavor to modify his physical defect by the careful selection of his coats. He should have his coats cut to give him as much length of leg as possible. A skilful tailor will know just what subtle changes and adjustments to make. The improvement in appearance and gain in height is pictured in sketch 88. The coat being shorter and the waist of the trousers being raised a trifle, the man's limbs seem longer, which is an improvement. Long lines tend to give elegance and grace in bearing. Another thing for the too robust type of man to consider is the style of his trousers. No. 87 hints what he must not choose. Such brazen plaids only make him appear offensively aggressive in size. Long, fine lines, such as shown in No. 88, give an impression of length and apparently lessen the width.

Too long lines, however, are almost as undesirable as too short ones. Over-tall, thin men sometimes make themselves look like telegraph poles or flagstaffs by wearing short coats that expose in a graceless way the whole length of their limbs. They suggest cranes and other fowl that give the impression of being " all legs."

When the legs are proportioned more like a stick of macaroni or a lead pencil than the shapely limbs of an Adonis, they appear exceedingly funny when surmounted by a short coat, such as pictured in No. 89. A famous general in the Civil War did not despise cotton as a fortification to protect him from the onslaught of the enemy. The over-tall, thin man, who is not unsuggestive of a picket, should not be ashamed to fortify himself with cotton or any other sort of padding that intelligent tailors keep in stock. He should build his shoulders up a bit and be generally, but most carefully and artistically, enlarged. His coat should be lengthened, as in sketch go, to cut off just as much of the longness of limb as can possibly be allowed without destroying artistic proportions. The very tall, thin man who unthinkingly wears

NO. 89

NO. 90

a very short coat should be brave and never turn his back to his enemy.

If he wears black and white check trousers and a short blue coat, he should travel with a screen. A man in just such a rig attracted no end of comment in a fashionable hotel. The caricaturing effect of his trousers and coat were unspeakably comical. The wearer had a face as grave as an undertaker's and the air of a serious-minded college professor; but he had the nondescript look of a scarecrow composed of whatever available garments could be obtained from the cast-off wardrobe of summer boarders in a farmhouse.

Coats assuredly have the power of making cartoons—living, jocular cartoons—of their wearers. It would hardly seem necessary to call attention to the fact that a man of huge dimensions should not wear a short coat, such as shown in sketch No. 91, yet his type is too frequently seen attired in this style. A man so dressed certainly seems the living exemplification of the definition of a jug, namely, " a vessel usually with a swelling belly, narrow mouth, and a handle, for holding liquors." It cannot be reiterated too often that a large, stout man should aim to acquire the distinction and dignity given by long lines. If his body is proportioned so he really has neither length of torso nor of limb he must pay more attention to the cut of his clothes and attain length in whatever artistic way he can. The long coat, as may be seen in sketch No. 92, not only apparently adds length but it conceals too protuberant curves.

NOS. 91 AND 92

Of course, character counts far more than clothes, we will all agree to that, but at first glance it is a man's clothes that impress people. Clothes affect our behavior somewhat. For instance, " When the young European emigrant, after a summer's labor puts on for the first time a new coat, he puts on much more. His good and becoming clothes put him on thinking that he must behave like people who are so dressed; and silently and steadily his behavior mends." Of course, there is an uplifting truth in George Herbert's maxim, " This coat with my discretion will be brave," yet, I am inclined to think that the majority of men who will stop to consider will agree with Emerson, who says, " If a man has not firm nerves and has keen sensibility, it is perhaps a wise economy to go to a good shop and dress himself irreproachably. He can then dismiss all care from his mind, and may easily find that performance an addition of confidence, a fortification that turns the scale in social encounters, and allows him to go gayly into conversations where else he had been dry and embarrassed. I am not ignorant,—I have heard with admiring submission the experience of the lady who declared 'that the sense of being perfectly well dressed gives a feeling of inward tranquillity which religion is powerless to bestow.'"

A popular clothier in New York, understanding this trait of his fellow-men, voices this same sentiment in his advertisement in this succinct way: " Seriously now. Have you ever stopped to think that if you wear good clothing it adds much to that independent, easy feeling you should have when you come in contact with other men?"

NO. 93

I think it was Lord Chesterfield who said: " A man is received according to his appearance, and dismissed according to his merits." There is a bit of truth in this we would all admit, I have no doubt, if we studied the question. Clothes affect our own poise, ease, and attitude toward others and the expression of others toward us, but, after all, we rely upon the man or woman instead of upon the impression we receive from the clothes. The garments, after we have noticed them in a superficial way, are chiefly interesting to us, because they are arch-betrayers of the physical and mental poise of the man. No matter what the cut of the cloth, no matter what *cachet* of a fashionable tailor a suit may have, or what its richness of material, the attitude " à la decadence" of No. 93 would make the best clothes in Christendom look shabby and unattractive.

This too familiar carriage of the American man makes one wish to have the power to reverse the faces—as Dante did those of the false prophets, so those who stand " à la decadence" might see what ridiculous figures they cut in drawing-room and street. The curved

44

backs and rounded-out shoulders would make fair-looking chests, and the flat chests would represent respectable-looking backs.

A man owes it to the spirit within him not to stand or walk in such an attitude. He should brace up and keep bracing up persistently, unremittently, until he attains a more manly bearing.

The wholly alive fellow pictured in sketch No. 94 would make homespun look elegant. His chest is forward. He does not sag in front at the waist, protruding his abdomen in not only an inartistic, but an unhealthy manner; but he strides masterfully forward with an air of inspiriting " aliveness." The perfect poise of his attitude is not unsuggestive of the Apollo Belvedere—the model for all men—a picture of which every college boy should have to place beside the prettiest girl in his collection of pretty girls, to constantly remind him to carry himself like a young god.